DATE DUE

Apr 27 84

994
Aus   Australia

Children of the World

Australia

For their help in the preparation of *Children of the World: Australia*, the editors gratefully thank Employment and Immigration Canada, Ottawa, Ont.; the US Immigration and Naturalization Service, Washington, DC; the Embassy of Australia (US), Washington, DC; the Australian Consulate General (US), Chicago; the International Institute of Wisconsin, Milwaukee; the United States Department of State, Bureau of Public Affairs, Office of Public Communication, Washington, DC, for unencumbered use of material in the public domain; and Justin McCarthy, M.D., of Perth, Australia, and St. Luke's Hospital, Racine, WI.

Library of Congress Cataloging-in-Publication Data

Yanagi, Akinobu, 1951-
    Australia.

    (Children of the world)
    Based on the original Japanese work by Akinobu Yanagi.
    Bibliography: p.
    Includes index.
    Summary: Presents the life of a young boy in New South
Wales describing his family, home, school, and amusements
and some of the traditions and celebrations of his country.

    1. Australia—Juvenile literature. 2. Children—
Australia—Juvenile literature. [1. Australia—Social
life and customs. 2. Family life—Australia]
I. Martin, Michael, 1948-   . II. Title. III. Series:
Children of the world (Milwaukee, Wis.)
DU96.Y36 1988   994.06'3   87-42617
ISBN 1-55532-247-6
ISBN 1-55532-222-0 (lib. bdg.)

North American edition first published in 1988 by
Gareth Stevens, Inc.
7317 West Green Tree Road Milwaukee, Wisconsin 53223, USA

This work was originally published in shortened form consisting of section I only.
Photographs and original text copyright © 1987 by Akinobu Yanagi.
First and originally published by Kaisei-sha Publishing Co., Ltd., Tokyo.
World English rights arranged with Kaisei-sha Publishing Co., Ltd.
through Japan Foreign-Rights Centre.

Copyright this format © 1988 by Gareth Stevens, Inc.
Additional material and maps copyright © 1988 by Gareth Stevens, Inc.

Typeset by Ries Graphics Ltd., Milwaukee.
Design: Laurie Bishop and Laurie Shock.
Map design: Kate Kriege.

1 2 3 4 5 6 7 8 9 92 91 90 89 88

Children of the World
Australia

Photography by
Akinobu Yanagi

Edited by
Michael Martin

Gareth Stevens Publishing
Milwaukee

. . . a note about *Children of the World:*

The children of the world live in fishing towns, Arctic regions, and urban centers, on islands and in mountain valleys, on sheep ranches and fruit farms. This series follows one child in each country through the pattern of his or her life. Candid photographs show the children with their families, at school, at play, and in their communities. The text describes the dreams of the children and, often through their own words, tells how they see themselves and their lives.

Each book also explores events that are unique to the country in which the child lives, including festivals, religious ceremonies, and national holidays. The *Children of the World* series does more than tell about foreign countries. It introduces the children of each country and shows readers what it is like to be a child in that country.

. . . and about *Australia:*

Scott is from New South Wales, in southeastern Australia. Australia is a country that is also its own continent. Scott's parents work at the local zoo, and the family house is actually located on the zoo grounds! Scott has overcome a difficult medical condition and enjoys his life in the zoo with his parents, his two sisters, and an assortment of friends.

To enhance this book's value in libraries and classrooms, comprehensive reference sections include up-to-date data about Australia's geography, demographics, language, currency, education, culture, industry, and natural resources. *Australia* also features a bibliography, research topics, activity projects, and discussions of such subjects as Canberra, the country's history, political system, ethnic and religious composition, and language.

The living conditions and experiences of children in Australia vary tremendously according to economic, environmental, and ethnic circumstances. The reference sections help bring to life for young readers the diversity and richness of the culture and heritage of Australia, a country that will impress North American readers with both the variety and familiarity of its many cultural facets. Of particular interest are discussions of the native Aboriginal culture that has made its presence felt in the language and traditions of Australia.

CONTENTS

LIVING IN AUSTRALIA:
  Scott, a Boy Growing Up in a Zoo 6

Scott's Home: The Western Plains Zoo 10
Scott's Parents at Work 14
Australia's Unique Wildlife 16
Relaxing at Home 18
Scott and Catherine's School 24
Dubbo — a Town on the Edge of the Plains 32
Shopping in Dubbo 38
At Play Around the House 40
A Trip to Lake Burrendong and Wellington 42

FOR YOUR INFORMATION: Australia 48

Official name and Capital 48
History 48
Currency 51
Government 51
Population and Ethnic Groups 52
Land 53
Climate 53
Map of Australia 54
Natural Resources 56
Industry and Agriculture 56
Art and Culture 56
Religion 58
Language 58
Education 58
Sports 59
Australia's Strange Animals 59
Canberra 60
Australians in North America 60
More Books About Australia 61
Glossary of Useful Australian Terms 61
Things to Do - Research Projects 61
More Things to Do - Activities 62
Index 63

The Lowe family: Scott (in the tree); his sister Maureen; his mother, Elly; his father, David; his sister Catherine (seated).

LIVING IN AUSTRALIA:
Scott, a Boy Growing Up in a Zoo

Scott Lowe is 10. He lives in Australia, a country about the same size as the continental United States. His home is in Dubbo, a city in the southeastern corner of the country. Scott lives with his sister Maureen, his parents, and his little sister Catherine.

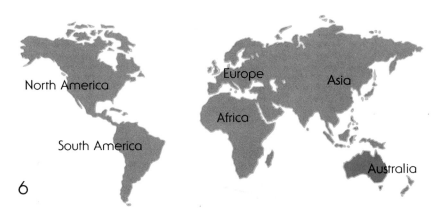

North America

South America

Europe

Asia

Africa

Australia

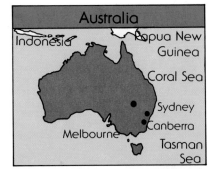

Australia

Indonesia

Papua New Guinea

Coral Sea

Sydney

Canberra

Melbourne

Tasman Sea

Scott likes to climb on the roof of his house.

Feeding a baby kangaroo.

Scott's parents work for the Western Plains Zoo, the largest zoo in Australia. Their home is actually inside the zoo. Scott enjoys living there because kangaroos and peacocks come to visit him. His favorite visitors, though, are ostrich-like birds called emus. Scott talks to the emus, and sometimes he draws pictures of them.

Dubbo from the air.

Scott's Home: The Western Plains Zoo

Visitors to the Western Plains Zoo rent bicycles to ride through the park and view the animals from all over the world. Scott lives near the area containing animals native to Australia. Since Scott is also from Australia, this arrangement suits him fine!

The people who designed the zoo tried very hard to provide the animals with a natural home. That is why there are no cages. Deep moats keep the animals in their proper places. Luckily for Scott, the kangaroos and emus are allowed to roam free!

A map of the zoo: "Here's where I live!"

A zoo tour bus.

Talking with a zookeeper.

Scott's favorite bird, by Scott.

With its forests, lakes, and open spaces, the Western Plains Zoo is an enjoyable place for both animals and humans. The road that goes around the park is more than three miles (five km) long, so there is plenty of room for everyone.

Scott and his sister Catherine like to talk with the zookeepers. It seems there's always something new to learn about the zoo and the animals that live in it. The children like to think of the zookeepers as their own private tour guides. Sometimes the children go off exploring on their own. They almost always find something interesting to investigate.

Emu eggs.

Playing with a giraffe.

There are about 2,000 animals living in the natural setting of the zoo. Although they have to be careful, Scott and Catherine enjoy playing with the animals that are friendly. Among the friendliest and gentlest are the giraffes. Scott and Catherine enjoy the ostriches, too.

The land that is used for animals takes up 740 sq acres (300 sq hectares) of land. But over half the entire land on which the zoo is located — another 988 sq acres (400 sq hectares) — is undeveloped. There are plans to make the zoo a bigger and better place. Scott's father is helping with those plans.

Scott's Parents at Work

Scott's father, David, is in charge of the zoo's maintenance department. He is responsible for the appearance of the grounds. His main job is caring for trees and plants, but he also has to make plans for expanding the zoo.

Before he started working at the zoo, Scott's father played Australian Rules professional football. David is retired from football now. But he is still a strong, active man who enjoys working outdoors. Whenever possible Scott likes to be near his dad. There are many things the two do together. Scott especially likes riding with his father on the zoo's tractor.

One of Scott's favorite things — riding on the tractor.

Trimming weeds.

14

David shows the children some seeds.

When Scott was born his legs were bowed. They were bent so badly that he had to have surgery and wear special shoes for a long time. It took eight years of treatment before he could walk normally. Scott's father worried a great deal when Scott was younger. He's quite relieved that his son is healthy now.

Scott's mother, Elly, works at a shop at the zoo. When school gets out for the day, Scott and Catherine like to visit her. Usually she gives them an ice cream treat.

Spotting a koala bear in a tree.

Two of Australia's national treasures: a koala bear . . .

. . . and some kangaroos.

Australia's Unique Wildlife

Australia is not only a country. It is also a continent as well as a huge island. Many of the animals that live on this island are found nowhere else in the world. Among them are the dingo, kangaroo, koala bear, and duck-billed platypus. Many of the strangest animals are marsupials (animals that carry their young in pouches). Kangaroos are marsupials.

A wild dog called a dingo.

Most marsupials are found south of the equator. One of the few marsupials also found in North America is the opossum. One day Scott and his sister discovered two baby opossums at the zoo's animal hospital. Their mother had been killed by a car, but the babies in her pouch survived. Scott and Catherine have "adopted" the babies, and the little opossums seem to enjoy climbing on the children's heads.

Playing with baby opossums.

A duck-billed platypus.

Relaxing at Home

When he played Australian professional football Scott's father was not home very much at all. Now when he gets through with work at the zoo he likes to relax by watching television with the family. Everyone enjoys having him around.

Scott enjoys looking through his father's many trophies and news clippings.

The family enjoys gathering together — and eating — in front of the television.

Scott likes to watch television, too. When he gets really interested in a program he tends to sit too close to the screen. Then his sisters have to remind him to move back. Maureen, Scott's older sister, is in high school. She enjoys sports and is on the volleyball team. Catherine goes to the same school as Scott. She's nine and in the 3rd grade.

Enjoying breakfast together on a holiday.

Everyone — all the children, at least! — helps out in the kitchen.

Scott shows off his games.

The clothes in Scott's closet give us an idea of Australia's weather.

Scott's soccer trophies.

The shelves in Scott's room are filled with toys and awards.

Three years ago, when Scott was finally able to wear regular shoes, he began playing soccer. His doctors told him that would help rebuild the strength in his legs. Since then he has won many trophies, but Scott still says the happiest moment in his life was when he won his first soccer trophy.

When Scott was younger his parents worried about his problems a lot. Scott doesn't remember much about those times. He's just glad to be better now.

Scott has his own room. In it he keeps his games, his soccer trophies, and stuffed animals that were given to him when he was younger. Usually he goes to bed around 9:30 p.m.

Taking a bath.

Getting ready for bed.

Maureen keeps busy helping with the cooking.

The family enjoys eating outside.

Barbecues are very popular in Australia. It does not often get cold in Australia, so there are plenty of days that are perfect for cooking out. Scott's family barbecues out in the yard once a week. Maureen and Catherine help their mother slice onions or take dishes out to the table while Scott's father does most of the cooking. Once in a while, Maureen lends a hand at the grill.

Sometimes Scott's stepbrother Michael joins them for a meal. Scott likes eating outdoors. The barbecued beef, chops, and sausage all seem to taste better outside. Scott's father has beer with his meal while the children have soda or fruit juice.

One of Scott's favorite meals: barbecued sausages and chops of steak, a salad, and a soft drink.

23

Scott and Catherine's School

Scott gets up around 7:00 a.m. and leaves for school after a breakfast of toast, corn flakes, and coffee, tea, or milk. He and his sisters first ride their bikes to the zoo entrance. Then they walk to a bus stop on the street. All three children ride the same bus to school. Dubbo West School is about 2½ miles (4 km) from the zoo. The bus lets Maureen off at her high school before it takes the younger children to their school.

Every Tuesday morning all the students gather in the playground for a weekly meeting. The principal makes announcements, talks about the previous week, and gives awards to students who have been doing especially well. Catherine has received quite a few of those awards.

Riding to the bus stop.

Scott's school.

DUBBO WEST PUBLIC SCHOOL PRIMARY DEPARTMENT

The bus stop.

The students gather for their meeting every Tuesday morning on the playground.

Raising the flag.

Teachers need to relax, too!

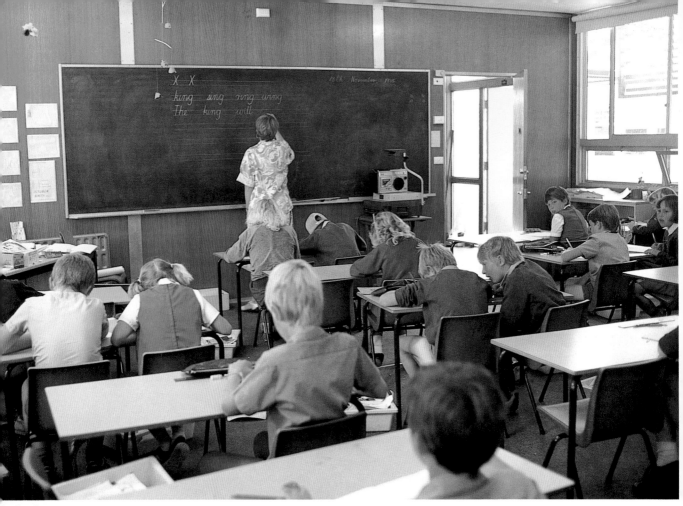

In class.

The students' desks have no drawers, so their books are kept in containers.

Scott's 5th grade class has 30 students. The school day begins at 9:30 a.m. and ends at 3:30 p.m. There is a break for lunch between noon and 1:00 p.m. Scott's favorite subject is math, but if he had a choice he would rather be playing sports than doing schoolwork.

Scott's mother wishes he would pay a little more attention to his studies. She'd like to see him go on to college. Scott's father is not quite as concerned about grades. He's just happy his son's physical problems are over.

In Scott's bag are his school supplies and lunch. His favorite lunch foods are sausage rolls, meat pie, and hot dogs. His mother has given up trying to interest him in anything else. Scott also loves apples. He eats three or four a day.

The school library.

The children leave their bags outside class.

The work of young artists hangs on the classroom wall.

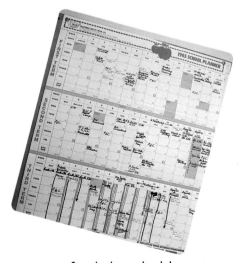
Scott's class schedules.

Scott's class. Scott is in the middle row, fifth from the left.

Some students take their photo session more seriously than others! 29

Scott's mother sends frozen fruit juice to school with him. When it's time to eat, the juice has thawed out. Scott eats lunch outside with his friends. Afterwards they play games. On Friday afternoons sports activities are scheduled after lunch. Soccer is Scott's favorite sport, but he also likes to play cricket, a game that originated in England.

Eating outside with friends.

Scott's lunch.

Discussing Friday's sports schedule with the principal.

The seasons in Australia are the opposite of those in the northern hemisphere. Scott's school year begins in late January or early February, and the six-week summer vacation starts in December. In September, during the Australian spring, schoolchildren all over the country help plant trees.

Playing cricket on a Friday afternoon.

Dubbo — A Town on the Edge of the Plains

Dubbo, Scott's hometown, has about 32,000 people. It lies in the Australian state of New South Wales, which is in southeastern Australia. Sydney is in New South Wales, too. However, the two cities are about 240 miles (400 km) apart, and Scott has been in Sydney only once in his life. With a population of four million people, Sydney is Australia's largest city.

Downtown Dubbo resembles the center of many small towns in North America.

The center of Dubbo on a clear, warm afternoon.

Though it is relatively small, Dubbo is a center for commerce. In this way Dubbo is not that different from towns its size in remote parts of North America. People from all over the region come into town to shop and play. Many come into Dubbo just to go to the zoo. As in many Australian cities, the stores in Dubbo stay open late on Thursday and Friday nights so people can shop when it is not so hot.

New South Wales is a very large state, and the land and climate often vary greatly from one part of the state to another. Sydney, for example, is near the ocean, while Dubbo is far inland. In fact, Dubbo is located at the far eastern end of the plains of central Australia. During the summer it is very hot and dry. Winter is a much more comfortable season since the temperatures almost always remain mild.

Dubbo's city hall.

Trees grow along the MacQuarrie River.

Many crops are grown on the plains around Dubbo. Among them are corn, oats, wheat, sunflowers, and cotton. Cattle and sheep are raised, too. Where animals are raised the farms tend to be very large. That is because the animals have to range over very large areas in order to find enough food to eat.

An aerial view of the plains around Dubbo.

Shopping in Dubbo

On Thursday nights Scott's whole family goes shopping in the new shopping center in Dubbo. The trip is supposed to be only for groceries, but the children have other things on their minds. Maureen is interested in clothes and records, Catherine looks for new dolls, and Scott keeps an eye out for games and sports equipment. Scott's mother usually tells the children that their shopping cart is just big enough to hold the things they really need and no more. This reasoning worked much better when the children were younger!

Dubbo's new shopping center.

Meats at the store.

Catherine explores the Christmas selection of toys.

Doing the weekly grocery shopping at a discount supermarket.

Loading the car. Catherine has been sampling some treats!

There is a bowling alley in the new shopping center, so tonight Scott's parents decide to take everyone bowling after the shopping is done. Scott enjoys himself, but when they finally get back home it is way past his bedtime. Scott wants to stay up and watch professional wrestling on television. But his father makes all the children go to bed.

At Play Around the House

There's lots at home to keep Scott and Catherine busy. They especially like to climb up on the roof of their house and jump down on the trampoline. Sometimes they play a game where one of them swings a jump rope and the other tries to jump over it without getting hit. Scott has a basketball net on a tree, and he can also practice cricket whenever he wants.

There is a swimming pool in the back yard that can't be used. Scott's father has promised the children he would fix it before summer vacation. Until then they will have to use the public swimming pool.

The public swimming pool.

Jumping off the roof!

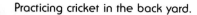

Practicing cricket in the back yard.

Scott and Catherine supervise as David waters the plants.

Scott's family is proud of their assortment of birds out in the yard.

Scott's father takes good care of the yard. He waters the grass, flowers, and vegetable garden. Outside there is a big birdcage with many pretty little birds in it. One day Scott and his sister go to the vegetable garden to pick something for the birds to eat. They are surprised to see a lizard resting on a cabbage plant. Scott tries to catch it, but it is too quick for him and runs away.

A lizard on a cabbage plant surprises Scott and Catherine one morning.

A Trip to Lake Burrendong and Wellington

The children are excited when their father decides to take them to a lake that is about an hour's drive from Dubbo. The name of the lake is Burrendong, and it is close to the town of Wellington. Their mother has to work, so she cannot join them. Lake Burrendong is a very big lake, and people come from long distances to boat and fish on it.

Lake Burrendong. Scott loves swimming in the big lake.

In dry Australia there are very few natural lakes. Lake Burrendong was created by building a dam on the MacQuarrie River. This dam is called the Burrendong Dam. To the people who come to the lake, it seems like an oasis in the desert. Around the lake grow eucalyptus, wattle, rubber plants, and sultan's parasol. In the spring, when the wildflowers bloom, it is a very beautiful place.

When they reach the lake Scott can't wait to jump in. It's a real treat for him to be in a body of water so much bigger than a swimming pool.

43

Inside Wellington Cave.

After a morning of swimming, Scott's father takes the children to nearby Wellington. One of the interesting things to do there is visiting Wellington Cave.

It is cool and dark inside. The guide says it is a limestone cave and explains how stalactites are formed. Later on he tries to scare everyone by turning off the lights for a few seconds.

Coming out of the cave.

After seeing Wellington Cave, the family visits a couple of local museums. One of them used to be a prison. Scott and Catherine look in the cells and try to imagine what it would be like to be a prisoner.

Wellington used to be known for its many outlaws, called *bushrangers* in Australia. The combination of Wellington's history and its prison museum makes it a fascinating place for Scott.

Looking inside a cell.

Catherine tries the stocks.

Inside a clock museum.

Eating lunch outside the clock museum.

The dolls move when you insert coins.

After their active day, Scott's father buys everyone sandwiches at a snack shop. While they eat, he mentions that tomorrow he will be going to the Taronga Zoo in Sydney. He will be gone a week. "Please take us along!" the children beg.

At first Scott's father says they can't come because it is supposed to be a business trip. After a little while, however, he decides it might be nice to have the children and their mother along. Scott is pleased and excited. On the way home from Wellington he and his sisters talk about the fun things they will do in Sydney.

FOR YOUR INFORMATION: Australia

Official name: Australia

Capital: Canberra

History

The Aborigines

Very little is known of Australia before the arrival of the first Europeans there. Somewhere between 25,000 and 40,000 years ago people from Asia began migrating south to Australia. These Aborigines, whose name means original inhabitants, gradually populated the entire continent. They lived not only in the fertile areas near the seacoasts but in the harsh deserts of the interior. For thousands of years, the Aborigines were isolated from the rest of the world. They developed distinctive physical characteristics and a unique culture. Most Aborigines have dark, brown skin and dark, wavy hair. Often, however, young children will have red or blonde hair that tends to darken as they get older.

Sydney, Australia's largest city.

Aborigines did not grow crops or raise domestic animals. Rainfall is very undependable in most of Australia and, as someone once said, you cannot ride or milk a kangaroo. Like the Indians of North America, the Aborigines roamed the land gathering edible fruits and vegetables and hunting. Their unique weapon was the boomerang, a fast, curved stick. A boomerang, when thrown, returns to the thrower. Aborigines lived in harmony with their environment.

Because food was often scarce, cooperation and sharing were highly valued. A successful hunter was expected to share his good fortune with the other members of the group. Over time the Aborigines developed a complex social system that was suited perfectly to survival in a harsh land. Unfortunately, that system offered very little protection against the arrival of the white man.

Discovery and Settlement

The first nonaboriginal visitors to Australia were probably sailors from China and Malaysia who occasionally landed on the north coast of Australia. The first European sighting was reported by the Dutch in the early part of the 17th century. In 1770, during a round-the-world voyage, Captain Cook explored the eastern coast and claimed the land for Britain.

The jails in Britain were crowded. People were imprisoned for debt and petty crimes like stealing food as well as serious criminal activities. Prior to the American Revolution, people convicted of crimes were often sentenced to be transported to the American colonies. As a new republic, the US declined to accept Britain's convicts, so Britain established a penal colony in Australia.

In 1787, just 17 years after Australia's discovery by Captain Cook, 11 ships set sail from Britain under the command of Captain Arthur Phillip. Of the 1,030 people on board, 736 were convicts.

On January 26, 1788, Captain Phillip's small fleet sailed into one of the world's finest natural harbors. The settlement that sprang up there eventually became the city of Sydney, and January 26 is celebrated as a holiday called Australian Day. The first few years, however, were hard ones. Rain was not dependable, and settlers had to learn what crops could grow in the Australian soil. Many colonists died before they learned how to survive in the strange new land.

To encourage emigration to Australia the British government offered free land to anyone willing to employ convicts. That strategy helped to begin populating the new colony, but many of the convicts were treated little better than slaves. Surprisingly few of them spent any time in prison. Most of them served their time at work and then became free men and women. A few convicts did escape into the wilderness and became outlaws. They came to be known as "bushrangers."

The transportation of convicts to Australia's mainland stopped in 1840. By that time

100,000 of them had been shipped from Britain. After serving their sentences in Australia, most of them became free and useful citizens.

Gold and Growth

Due to poor economic conditions in Europe, the number of free settlers increased after 1840. That increase turned into a flood after 1851, when gold was discovered in Victoria and New South Wales. Over the next 10 years another 600,000 people arrived in Australia.

Another factor in the growth of Australia was the development of the wool industry. In the late 18th century Captain John MacArthur experimented with the breeding of Merino sheep. These sheep from the dry plains of Spain proved to be well suited for Australia's hot climate. In time, they would help Australia become the world's leading producer of wool.

Federation and the First World War — the Anzacs and Gallipoli

The Commonwealth of Australia came into existence on January 1, 1901. On that date the six former colonies of New South Wales, Tasmania, Western Australia, South Australia, Victoria, and Queensland joined together in a federation of states to form modern Australia. The new country also had two federal territories — the Australian Capital Territory (site of the nation's capital) and the sparsely populated Northern Territory.

When World War I began in 1914, Australia joined Britain in opposing Germany. Soldiers from Australia and New Zealand combined to form the Australian and New Zealand Army Corps. These men soon came to be called Anzacs. Their first battle cannot be considered a victory, but it is probably the most widely-honored event in Australian history.

On April 25, 1915, the Anzacs were transported on ships to a place called Gallipoli. Gallipoli was a finger of land that overlooked an important waterway near Turkey. It was guarded by Turkish soldiers who were allies of Germany. The Anzacs faced overwhelming odds in fighting their way ashore because they were mistakenly landed in a heavily-defended area. Thousands of Australians and New Zealanders were killed, but somehow the survivors fought their way up into the steep hills above the landing area. They remained in those hills for the next eight months, unable to move forward and unwilling to leave.

Finally, in November, the decision was made to evacuate the troops. Each night, under cover of darkness, soldiers were secretly taken away on ships. In the end there were only a handful of men left to defend the position. They ran from gun to gun trying to fool the Turks into thinking there were still many soldiers left. Their efforts were successful. Not until after the last Anzac soldier had left did the Turks realize that an evacuation had been under way.

Although the evacuation was a success, the landing itself was a failure. Nothing at all was gained by the loss of 13,000 Anzac lives. Still, Australians had reason to be proud of their countrymen. Australian troops had fought bravely in an impossible situation that was not their fault. The anniversary of the landing at Gallipoli is now celebrated as a national holiday called Anzac Day.

The Second World War

Early in World War II, during the fighting in the Pacific, it seemed the Japanese would invade northern Australia. Australia called its troops back from Europe to defend against the expected invasion. During this time the Australians began working closely with US military forces. One of the turning points of the war was the Battle of the Solomon Islands. Australian scouts, operating deep within Japanese-held territory, radioed word of enemy movements to the Americans. They were given much of the credit for the eventual victory. Thousands of US soldiers and sailors visited Australia for the first time during the war. The friendship and cooperation between the two countries has continued to this day.

Australia Today

Australia has changed greatly since the end of WW II. Because of an extensive immigration program, the population has more than doubled. Today, one out of four Australians was born overseas. During the first 50 years of Australia's existence immigration was strictly limited to white Europeans. That policy was eventually abolished, and Australia has become a much more diverse society.

Currency

The Australian currency system is identical to systems used in Canada and the United States, with 100 cents in an Australian dollar. Each denomination, 1, 5, 10, 20, and so on, is a different color.

Government

The federal government of Australia is based in Canberra, the nation's capital. Like the US Congress, the Australian Parliament has two chambers: the House of Representatives and the Senate. The political party with the majority in the House heads the government and chooses a Prime Minister. Australia pioneered voting by secret ballot. People who fail to vote have to pay a fine.

A difficult problem facing the government has been the immigration issue. Australia is almost as large as the United States, but it has only about the same number of people as Texas. Some Australians fear that their country will change drastically if too many newcomers are allowed in. Other Australians believe that if their country is going to continue to grow and prosper it will need the help of many more people. So far, the government has tried to find a balance between these two views. Immigration is increasing, but special care has been taken to provide newly-arrived immigrants with any help they might need to become productive members of Australian society.

Population and Ethnic Groups

An Urban Nation

More than 16 million people live in Australia. Although Australia is one of the most sparsely populated nations on Earth, it is also one of the most urbanized because most people live in the cities. Sydney, with 4 million people, and Melbourne, with 2.5 million, are the country's two largest cities.

Only 15% of the population lives in rural areas. Much of this rural area is remote and isolated because Australia's cities are few and very far between. Some cities are connected mainly by train lines. Across the Nullarbor Plain from Port Augusta to Kalgoorlie, the Tea and Sugar train runs once a week. It brings food and supplies to the people who live along the way. These are mostly railroad workers, rabbit hunters, and prospectors and their families. The train pulls a supermarket car, a social services car, and fresh water tank cars. At regular intervals other cars hook up: a department store car, a paymaster's car, a church car, and others. The train used to carry hospital cars, a movie and theater car, and a tuberculosis and dental car in the olden days of this 70-year-old run. Today people take the train to larger cities for medical care, and the Tea and Sugar brings video movies instead of a movie theater.

The Aborigines

Asians and Aborigines are Australia's two largest ethnic groups, though 95% of the population is of European background. When Europeans arrived in Australia 300,000 Aborigines lived there. Contact with the white man proved disastrous for them. White settlers did not understand or care that, even though the Aborigines did not plant crops, they needed the land to live off of. White men forced them off the good land and took over their food and water sources. In some areas Aborigines could be shot on sight.

Those Aborigines who did not starve or die of European diseases moved back into the remote areas of the country. For a while it seemed as if all the Aborigines would die off. Their numbers dropped to a low of 45,000 earlier in this century. In recent years their numbers have been increasing and they now make up about 1.0% of the population. Since World War II the government has provided funds to teach English and job skills to Aborigines living in cities. In the northern and central parts of Australia there are places where Aborigines retain many of their tribal ways. The government has been helping these people buy up the land they live on so they can continue to live in their traditional ways.

The Aborigines are still Australia's poorest minority, and much work needs to be done. But at least the government is now consulting with Aborigine leaders to try to find the best way to ensure their future as individuals and as a people.

Land

Australia is the world's sixth largest country and the only one that is also both a continent and an island. It is bordered on the south and west by the Indian Ocean and on the east by the Coral and Tasman Seas. To the north are straits of water which separate it from Indonesia and New Guinea.

The western two-thirds of the country consists mostly of a flat, irregular plateau. The center of Australia is especially flat, barren, and dry. There are, however, a few mountain ranges in Australia. The largest of these is the Great Dividing Range, which runs north to south almost the entire length of the eastern coast. As mountain ranges go it is not a particularly tall one. Its highest point, Mount Kosciusko, rises to a height of 7,310 feet (2,228 m). Australians call the undeveloped lands on the inland side of the coastal mountains the "Outback."

The Australian Alps in the country's southeast corner are tall enough to be snowcovered in winter. Major ski areas operate there from June until October. Other smaller mountain ranges are located near the center of Australia and in the west. Ayers Rock, the world's largest rock, rises 1,100 feet (335 m) above the vast open desert of central Australia. The Aborigines consider Ayers Rock a sacred place.

Off the northeast coast of Australia lies one of the great natural wonders of the world. The Great Barrier Reef parallels the coast of Queensland for 1,250 miles (2,000 km). Besides its beautiful coral formations, the reef is home to hundreds of species of fish and sea animals. Tourists from all over the world come to visit.

Ayers Rock: the largest one-piece rock in the world.

Climate

Because it is such a large country, there is a great range of climates in Australia. It is a long way from the tropical rain forests of northern Queensland to the snow-covered mountains of Tasmania. That difference, however, is somewhat misleading. With the exception of the lands along the eastern and northern coasts, most of the country is hot and dry. The hottest temperatures have been recorded in northwest Australia. Marble Bar once recorded a maximum temperature of 100°F (38°C) or more for 162 consecutive days. For many Australians, winter is a much more comfortable season than summer.

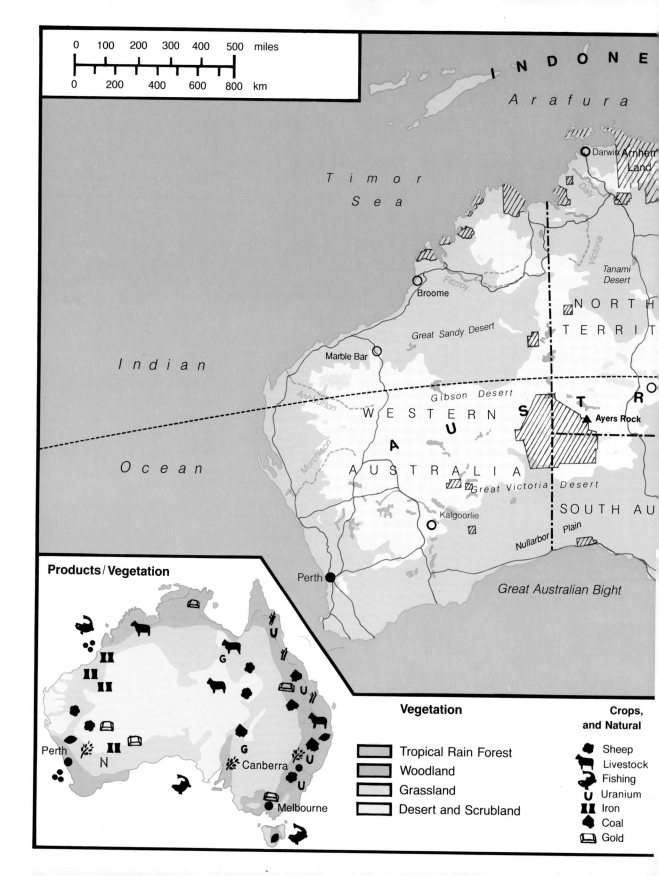

INDONE

Arafura

Timor
Sea

Darwin Arnhem
Land

Daly

Tanami
Desert

NORTH
TERRIT

Broome

Fitzroy

Great Sandy Desert

Indian

Marble Bar

Ashburton

Gibson Desert

WESTERN

S T R O

Ayers Rock

Ocean

Murchison

A

U

AUSTRALIA

Great Victoria Desert

SOUTH AU

Kalgoorlie

Nullarbor Plain

Perth

Great Australian Bight

Scale

0 100 200 300 400 500 miles

0 200 400 600 800 km

Products / Vegetation

Perth

N

G

G

Canberra

Melbourne

Vegetation

	Tropical Rain Forest
	Woodland
	Grassland
	Desert and Scrubland

**Crops,
and Natural**

Sheep
Livestock
Fishing
U Uranium
II Iron
Coal
Gold

AUSTRALIA – Political and Physical

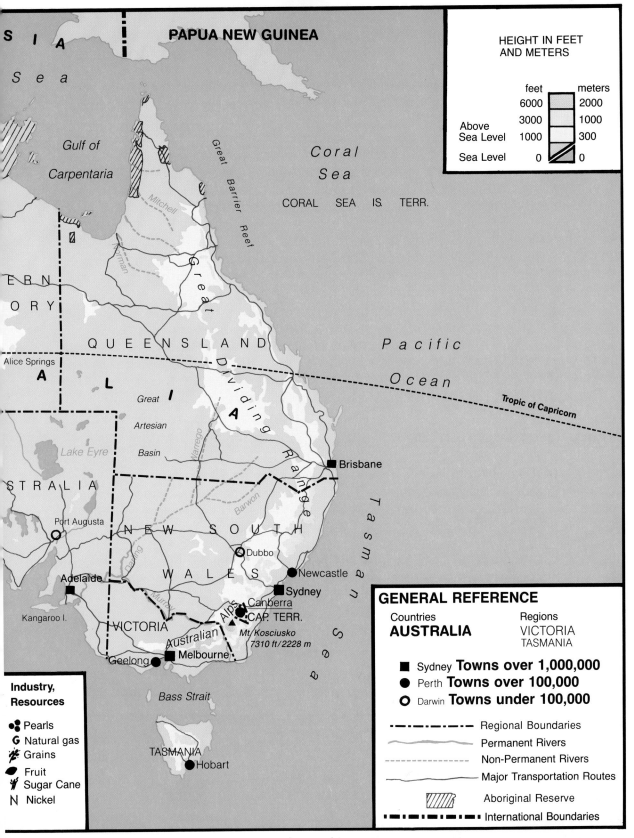

PAPUA NEW GUINEA

S I A

Sea

Gulf of

Carpentaria

Coral

Sea

CORAL SEA IS. TERR.

Mitchell

Great Barrier Reef

Flinders

HEIGHT IN FEET
AND METERS

	feet		meters
	6000		2000
Above	3000		1000
Sea Level	1000		300
Sea Level	0		0

ERN

ORY

QUEENSLAND

Pacific

Alice Springs

A

L

Ocean

Tropic of Capricorn

Great

Artesian

Basin

I

A

Warrego

Lake Eyre

● Brisbane

STRALIA

NEW   SOUTH

○ Port Augusta

Barwon

Tasman

○ Dubbo

W A L E S

● Newcastle

Adelaide

■ Sydney

Darling

Canberra

● Geelong

Kangaroo I.

VICTORIA

Murray

Alps

Australian

CAP. TERR.

▲ Mt Kosciusko
7310 ft/2228 m

■ Melbourne

Sea

Bass Strait

TASMANIA

● Hobart

Industry, Resources

● Pearls
G Natural gas
⚘ Grains
🍒 Fruit
🌾 Sugar Cane
N Nickel

GENERAL REFERENCE

Countries
AUSTRALIA

Regions
VICTORIA
TASMANIA

■ Sydney **Towns over 1,000,000**
● Perth **Towns over 100,000**
○ Darwin **Towns under 100,000**

Regional Boundaries
Permanent Rivers
Non-Permanent Rivers
Major Transportation Routes
Aboriginal Reserve
International Boundaries

Natural Resources

Australia is one of the world's major producers of minerals and metals. Minerals tend to occur in old rocks, and Australia has some of the oldest rocks in the world. Many of the country's mineral riches lie close to the surface, hidden under a light covering of sand or soil. Titanium and other rare metals have even been found in beach sand.

Australia has large deposits of coal, bauxite, gold, diamonds, and uranium. It is one of the major producers of energy resources as the world's largest exporter of coal, and it exports large quantities of uranium and natural gas. Oil has also been discovered in Australia, and increasing amounts are being exported.

The Australian Alps in the southeast are one of the few areas in the country that get dependable amounts of rain and snow. The Snowy Mountain hydroelectric scheme was built to take advantage of that fact. It is Australia's greatest engineering feat and one of the world's largest irrigation and power projects.

The project took 25 years to complete. It uses a complicated series of dams, pumping stations, and tunnels to transport water from one side of the Great Dividing Range to the other. Water that used to run down the mountains and into the sea is now taken over the mountains and used to irrigate lands that were too dry to grow crops. The Snowy Mountain project also provides electric power.

Industry and Agriculture

More than a million of Australia's 6.5 million workers are employed in manufacturing jobs. Some of the country's important industries are mining, chemicals, oils, textiles, and the aerospace industry. More than a million people visit Australia every year, and tourism is the single largest industry.

Australia is a major producer and exporter of agricultural products. Grains, milk and cheese, sugar, and fruits are all produced in large quantities there. The raising of livestock is also a major agricultural industry in Australia. About 90% of the agricultural land is in its natural state and is suitable only for light grazing by cattle or sheep. The country is the world's leading producer of wool and the second largest producer of meat. Many of the steaks and hamburgers eaten in Canada and the United States come from Australia.

Arts and Culture

A Developing Culture

In the first hundred years of European settlement most Australians had little time to devote to art. That began to change just before the turn of the century. Painters like

Tom Roberts and Arthur Streeton developed a distinctive style based on Aboriginal art and the unique landscapes of their country.

Perhaps the most easily recognized building in all of Australia is the Sydney Opera House. It is an example of one of the worst guesses ever made as to how much a project would cost — it was supposed to cost $7 million and ended up costing $102 million. But it is one of the most striking buildings ever built — a magnificent place to view an opera, symphony, play, or film.

In recent years the Australian filmmakers have produced many films which have attracted worldwide attention. Among them are movies like *The Year of Living Dangerously, Gallipoli, My Brilliant Career,* and *The Road Warrior.*

Aboriginal Arts

The art of the Australian Aborigines includes rock paintings, painted objects, engravings on weapons and tools, and bark paintings. Perhaps the most striking works of Aboriginal art are the cave paintings found by the thousands across northern Australia. Some are believed to be more than 5,000 years old.

In the caves of the northwest are found the *Wandijinas.* These are huge, spooky-looking figures painted white. They have black eyes and black noses but no mouths. According to traditional belief, the *Wandijinas* themselves made these paintings at the very beginning of time. In western Arnhem Land are paintings unlike any others in the world. These "X-ray" paintings are of animals, birds, fish, and reptiles. They show not only the bodies of these creatures, but their skeletons and internal organs.

Bark painting is the form of Aborigine art most familiar to the average Australian. Bark paintings were apparently first used as decorations for the interiors of Aborigine shelters along the seacoasts. A typical bark painting might tell the story of an expedition to collect seagull eggs. Bark paintings have become quite popular and many people collect them. Some Aborigines earn extra money by making bark paintings to sell to tourists. More authentic examples of bark paintings can be seen in Australia's major art museums.

The ancient Aborigines had very few musical instruments. One of them was the didjeridoo. People played the didjeridoo by blowing through a hollowed-out branch or tree trunk to produce a deep, throbbing tone. Another sound-making instrument made by the Aborigines was the bull-roarer. Bull-roarers are pieces of wood attached to a string. When whirled through the air they make a sound that was said to be the voice of a great spirit.

Because their ancient culture did not have writing, the Aborigines learned other ways to express themselves. The Aborigine word *corroboree* originally meant a celebration where stories were told through music and dance. A few years ago some white men who were studying the Aborigines observed a corroboree at

Barrow Creek. As they watched the dancers they noticed that one of them was stopping in front of the other dancers, looking each of them over closely, then pretending to write in a notebook. It did not take the white men very long to realize they were being shown how silly they appeared to the rest of the tribe.

Religion

People from all the world's major religions worship in Australia, but three out of four Australian church-goers are Christians. The largest denominations are Roman Catholic and Episcopalian, also known as the Church of England.

The Aborigines' complex and unusual religion has attracted interest from scholars all over the world. One of the more intriguing concepts is Dreamtime. The Aborigines believe that when the world began time was split into regular time and Dreamtime. It is possible to enter Dreamtime by dreaming or, sometimes, by going into a trance. They believe that their ancestors and other mythical beings live forever in Dreamtime and that it is possible to go to them and talk to them during sleep.

Language

The official language of Australia is English, and spelling generally follows the British form. There are many phrases and slang words used by Australians that North Americans would have trouble understanding.

When the first Europeans arrived in Australia the Aborigines spoke at least 260 closely related languages. Very few of those languages survive today, but a number of them have been studied. Those studies have shown the aboriginal languages to be totally unrelated to any of the world's languages. That is further evidence that the Aborigines were separated from other cultures for a long time.

Education

Most Australian children attend some form of preschool before the age of six. Except in Tasmania, all children have to attend school from 6-15 (16 in Tasmania). The school year runs from February through early December. There are holidays in May and August, and a six-week summer vacation in December and January. Two-thirds of Australian children attend free government schools.

The Australian government places a high value on educating its children. There are many special programs to teach them the skills necessary to succeed in life. In the capital city of each state are correspondence schools. They serve children who cannot attend regular schools because of distance or physical disability.

Along with correspondence schools, children in the Australian Outback are educated by the "school of the air." The school of the air teaches over short-wave radio. Students talk twice a day to their teachers while other students from tiny towns and sheep and cattle stations listen in. The programs help the children make contact with others, because the great distances of the Outback make it very hard for kids to get together.

There are also special programs to teach English to non-English-speaking children. These programs are for Aborigine children and children of recent immigrants. In addition, funds are provided for English-speaking children who would like to learn another language after normal school hours.

Sports

Australia is a very sports-minded country. Sports that are popular with children include cricket, swimming, Australian Rules football, soccer, rugby, basketball, and tennis. And these sports are not all just for boys. Over a million girls and women regularly compete in a variety of sports.

Even in winter it is rarely too cold to enjoy outdoor activities in Australia. That is one reason why so many Australians play golf or tennis. Australian golfers and tennis players are among the best in the world. In 1971, an Aboriginal 19-year-old woman named Evonne Goolagong won the women's tennis title at Wimbledon. She won the title again in 1980. There have also been a number of Australian men who have won at Wimbledon, such as Pat Cash in 1987.

Australian Rules football is a special form of football played only in Australia. It is a very rough but popular game. Cricket is Australia's most popular summer team sport, both to play and to watch. Horse racing is another favorite activity. All the major Australian cities have race tracks.

Eighty-five percent of Australians live within 60 miles (100 km) of the ocean, so it is not surprising that swimming and sailing are extremely popular. One of the nation's proudest moments was the 1956 Melbourne Olympics. Australians won 13 gold medals then, most of them in swimming. Another proud moment came in 1983, when the Australia II became the first foreign yacht in 132 years to win the America's Cup from the United States. The US won it back in 1987.

Australia's Strange Animals

Australia has been geographically separated from the rest of the world for a long time, and the animals that developed there may seem very strange. The largest group of strange animals belongs to the marsupial family. They range in size from kangaroos nine feet (three m) long to phalangers (a kind of squirrel) whose babies are so small they cannot be seen without a magnifying glass.

There are about 125 kinds of marsupials in Australia, and many of them have funny names. Besides kangaroos, there are wombats, numbats, wallabies, koala bears, Tasmanian devils, and rabbit-eared bandicoots. Tasmanian devils are short, stocky animals with sharp teeth and strong jaws. They are about the size of a small dog. Tasmanian devils are extinct on mainland Australia, but some survive in remote areas of Tasmania.

Possibly the strangest animal in the world is the duck-billed platypus. It has a tail like a beaver, a bill like a duck, and webbed feet — and it is covered with thick fur. Besides the spiny anteater (which also lives in Australia), it is the only mammal that lays eggs. The first scientists who saw a platypus had trouble believing it was a real animal!

There are many colorful birds in Australia.

Canberra

Canberra, the capital of Australia, lies on a plain at the foot of the Australian Alps. It has a population of about 250,000 and, like Washington, DC, it was designed as a capital city. In 1911 the Australian government announced a worldwide competition to design their new capital. The winner of that competition was a Chicago architect named Walter Burley Griffin.

As part of his design for the new city, Griffin decided to dam the Molonglo River to create an artifical lake. Lake Burley Griffin is 22 miles (35 km) in circumference and is surrounded by many parks. There were no trees in Canberra when Griffin began work, so he also planted thousands of trees. The city is now the home of Australian National University, two major libraries, foreign embassies, and many governmental organizations.

Australians in North America

Being from a country of city dwellers, most Australians in the US and Canada settle in large cities. Many are professionals, especially doctors, scientists, and business executives, and California is a popular new home. About 1,500 Australians have immigrated each year to the US since 1976. Canada receives about 230 a year. Though most Australians move to England rather than the US or Canada, many come to visit each year. In recent years, more than 85,000 visited Canada and 200,000 visited the US for pleasure or business.

More Books About Australia

Here are some more books about Australia. If they interest you, check your library. They may be helpful in doing research for the "Things to Do" projects.

An Aboriginal Family. Browne (Lerner)
Australia. Santrey (Troll)
Looking at Australia. Henderson (Harper & Row)
Red Earth, Blue Sky: The Australian Outback. Rau (Crowell Junior Books)
Salt River Times. Mayne (Greenwillow)
Wallaby Creek. Powzyk (Lothrop, Lee & Shepard)

Glossary of Useful Australian Terms

English is the national language of Australia, but there are many Australian words that would not be familiar to people from other English-speaking countries. Some of them are listed below along with some Aboriginal words that have gained wide use in Australian society.

arvo	afternoon
billabong	a pond left when a stream dries up
brolly	an umbrella
corroboree	Aboriginal ceremonial dance; a celebration or meeting
cozzie	a bathing suit
damper	an unleavened bread usually cooked in a campfire
fair dinkum	the real thing; absolutely true; genuine
G'day	Hello; Welcome
ice block	a popsicle, also called "icy pole"
jackaroo	a young male ranch hand
jillaroo	a young female ranch hand
jumbuck	sheep
lollies	candy
mate	a friend
milk bar	soda fountain
mustering	rounding up sheep or cattle
Pommie	an Englishman
station	a large ranch
sandshoes	sneakers
Ta	Thank you

Things to Do — Research Projects

For many years, the Aborigines suffered in much the same way that other native peoples have at the hands of European colonizers. Today, the Aborigines are still

Australia's poorest minority. But at least public attitudes have changed, and the government is consulting with Aborigines themselves to find the best way to improve their lot in Australian life. As you read about Australia, keep in mind the importance of current facts. That is why current newspapers and magazines are useful sources of information for research projects. Two publications your library may have will tell you about recent articles on many topics:

The Reader's Guide to Periodical Literature
The Children's Magazine Guide

For accurate answers to questions about Australia today, look up *Australia* in these two publications.

1. Compare how white immigrants to North America and Australia treated the people they found living there. What is being done now in these countries to restore what was taken from the native populations?

2. How do the immigration policies of the US or Canada compare with Australia's? Are there racial quotas? Nationality quotas? Labor quotas? How have these policies affected the development of the population?

3. What is Australian Rules football? How is it different from US and Canadian professional football?

More Things to Do — Activities

These projects are designed to encourage you to think more about Australia. They offer ideas for interesting group or individual projects for school or home.

1. Take a trip to a zoo or nature preserve. What animals do you see that live in both North America and Australia? Which, if any, are strictly Australian?

2. Find out more about the culture of the Aborigines. Two features you may have read of or seen in the movies are Dreamtime and the Walkabout.

3. The Australian national anthem, "Waltzing Matilda," is not the kind of somber music typical of many national anthems. Find a record or tape of it in your library or record store. Learn the words *and* their meaning. You probably won't understand it without doing some research, even though it's in English.

4. For a pen pal in Australia, write to these people:

International Pen Friends   Be sure to tell them what country you want
P.O. Box 65   your pen pal to be from. Also, include
Brooklyn, New York 11229   your full name, address, and age.

Index

Aboriginal art, 57-58
Aboriginal religion, 58
Aborigines, 48-49, 52-53, 57-58, 59
agriculture, 35, 49, 50, 56
America's Cup, 59
animals, 7, 10-13, 16-17, 35, 41, 59-60
Anzac Day, 50
Anzacs, 50
art, 56-58
Asia, 48
Asians, 52
Australian Alps, 52, 56, 60
Australian Capital Territory, 50
Australian Day, 49
Australian National University, 60
Australian Rules football, 14, 18, 59
Ayers Rock, 53

bark painting, 57
boomerang, 49
Britain, 49-50, 60
Burrendong Dam, 43
bushrangers, 45, 49

California (US), 60
Canada (see also North America), 51, 56, 60
Canberra, 48, 51, 60
Cash, Pat, 59
Chicago (US), 60
China, 49
Church of England, 58
climate, 34, 49, 50, 53
Commonwealth of Australia, 50
Cook, Captain, 49
Coral Sea, 53
currency, 51

dance, 57-58
Dreamtime, 58
Dubbo, 6, 8-9, 32-35, 38-39, 42
Dubbo West School, 24-31
Dutch, 49

economy (see agriculture, industry, and natural resources)

education, 24-31, 58-59
Episcopalian, 58
ethnic groups, 48, 52
Europeans, 48-50, 51, 52, 56

farming (see agriculture)
food, 22-23, 24, 27, 30, 41
football, Australian Rules, 14, 18, 59

Gallipoli, 50-51
Germany, 50, 51
gold, 50, 56
Goolagong, Evonne, 59
government, 51-52
Great Barrier Reef, 53
Great Dividing Range, 53, 56
Griffin, Walter Burley, 60

immigrants, Australian, in North America, 60
immigration, 48-50, 51-52, 59
Indian Ocean, 53
Indonesia, 53
industry, 56

Japan, 51

Kalgoorlie, 52

Lake Burley Griffin, 60
Lake Burrendong, 42-43
land, 45, 53
language, 58, 59

MacArthur, Captain John, 50
MacQuarrie River, 43
Malaysia, 49
Marble Bar, 53
Melbourne, 52
minerals, 56
Molonglo River, 60
Mt. Kosciusko, 53
music, 57-58

natural resources, 56
New Guinea, 53
New South Wales, 32, 50

New Zealand, 50-51
North America (*see also* Canada *and* United States), 17, 49, 58
Northern Territory, 50
Nullarbor Plain, 52

Outback, 53, 59

Phillip, Captain Arthur, 49
population, 52-53
Port Augusta, 52
prisons, 45, 49-50

Queensland, 50, 53

religion, 58
Roberts, Tom, 57
Roman Catholic, 58

schools (*see* education)
sheep, 50, 56
shopping, 33, 38-39
Snowy Mountain Project, 56
South Australia, 50
Spain, 50
sports, 14, 18, 19, 20-21, 26, 30, 31, 40, 59
Streeton, Arthur, 57
Sydney, 32, 46-47, 49, 52
Sydney Opera House, 57

Taronga Zoo, 46
Tasmania, 50, 53, 58, 60
Tasman Sea, 53
Tea and Sugar Train, 52
Turkey, 50-51

United States (*see also* North America), 6, 49, 51, 56, 59, 60

Victoria, 50

Wandjinas, 57
Washington, DC (US), 60
Wellington, 42, 44-47

Wellington Cave, 44-45
Western Australia, 50
Western Plains Zoo, 7, 10-17
World War I, 50
World War II, 51, 52